Dead to Rights
A Circularity of Glosas

Dead to Rights

A Circularity of Glosas

by

Alain C. Dexter

Greyhart Press

www.greyhartpress.com

Dead to Rights

A Circularity of Glosas

Published by Greyhart Press

ISBN: 978-1-909636-01-9

Also available as

Kindle eBook

ePUB eBook

To G.C.,

my glosera,

with love

Contents

1. South: Innocence

2. West: Chaos

3. North: Wisdom

4. East: Higher Ground

5. Center: Mastery

Foreword

"Glosa: isn't that the floor wax they banned?"

The British-Canadian humourist, whose name you'd recognize, was plying his trade as assiduously as I when we happened to share an elevator in Montego Bay at the 1st Annual PFFF! (Poetry for the Fun & Fearless Festival!) a few months ago.

"Why, yes it is," I said, playing along. "I hope you didn't buy any."

"Are you kidding? My wife was a distributor. Our floors were so buffed, you couldn't take a step without cracking your head open. We had to hand out helmets at the front door for guests."

We both laughed with that hic-cough of anxiety common to successful writers, artists and musicians who never quite trust the dream they're living. But in a larger sense, my new friend had nailed it. The glosa is a poetry form buffed to a gleam so reflective, you don't even know, your first stanza in, that you've been concussed.

Glosas first entered our collective consciousness about nine hundred years ago, during what some call the Dark Ages, when European kings were warlords, dukes their boot-licking lackeys, and commoners fodder for whatever new war machines were being tested. The biggest employer in those days was the Crusades.

In the midst of that lunacy were a group of poet-musicians known as troubadours, whose job it was to keep royals and their courtiers entertained, to pass intelligence from dukedom to dukedom, and to assuage terror in the villages and on the treacherous, bandit-riddled byways between them. Like their in-house peers, the jesters, troubadours, quite literally, survived by their wits.

The competition to create new, exciting poetry forms was fierce. Some, like the ghazal, were already well established in the Persian and Arab worlds. Sonnets, those tight little fourteen-liners with intricate rhyme schemes, came later, and, like most poetic forms, served the medieval equivalent of corporate branding. Those in the know could tell you which kingdom or city-state a sonnet came from—Sicily, Venice, Genoa—by its themes and end rhymes. Those who didn't know—well, you didn't dare not know.

The glosa, of which you will find eighteen in this book, originated in 12th century Spain. The verb, *glosar*, means both to gloss and to sum up. The *glosero* or *glosera*—female troubadours did exist—would pay tribute to master poets by "borrowing" four lines of their poetry. These served as the opening or crown stanza. The following four ten-line stanzas were crafted by the *glosero*; nine lines were his own, the tenth came from the opening quatrain. To blend the originating work with the new, the poet rhymed the end words of lines six and nine with the master poet's tenth.

If my explanation scrambled your brain cells, don't worry. My first experience with glosas seventeen years ago overthrew everything

I believed about time, space, life, love, reality, potential, possibility and truth. And I'd only written one!

Fortunately, reading glosas is not nearly so traumatic. They deliver like a compact short story, in stereo; they're a poetic high energy drink, double shot espresso of verse. You can read one glosa and read it again several times to experience a kaleidoscope effect of something new with each reread. Or you can take in a whole wallop of them and begin to sense the underlying structure that gives the glosa its . . . well, glisten.

Listen. Space does not permit me to share the whole story of how glosas entered my life. As a professor of English literature who should have known better, I remained stubbornly resistant to their allure for years, and that is my loss. However, you can read the biographical account in Elaine Stirling's novella of horror and good medicine, *Dead Edit Redo*. You will also meet the author of seventeen of the glosas in this book, who would prefer to remain unnamed, and learn the tragic tale of the eighteenth.

This new edition of *Dead to Rights: A Circularity of Glosas* has been arranged in the clockwise order of the Medicine Wheel, with each of the glosas corresponding to a cardinal direction and concluding with the central fire of mastery. The Medicine Wheel is the fundamental teaching modality of Native Americans and First Nations people of Canada. Mystics and the indigenous people of every continent—the Celts, Sufis, Maya, the Australian aborigine— understand that we live circular, spiraling lives. Those of us who grew up with the Eurocentric, linear, left brain view of things are only now starting to admit the larger picture.

My deepest gratitude goes out to those who made this book possible, and in the manner of glosas, Medicine Wheels and circularities everywhere, my thanks cycles back to each and every one of you.

Alain C. Dexter, Ph.D.
Professor of Poetry
Brougham College
August 8, 2012

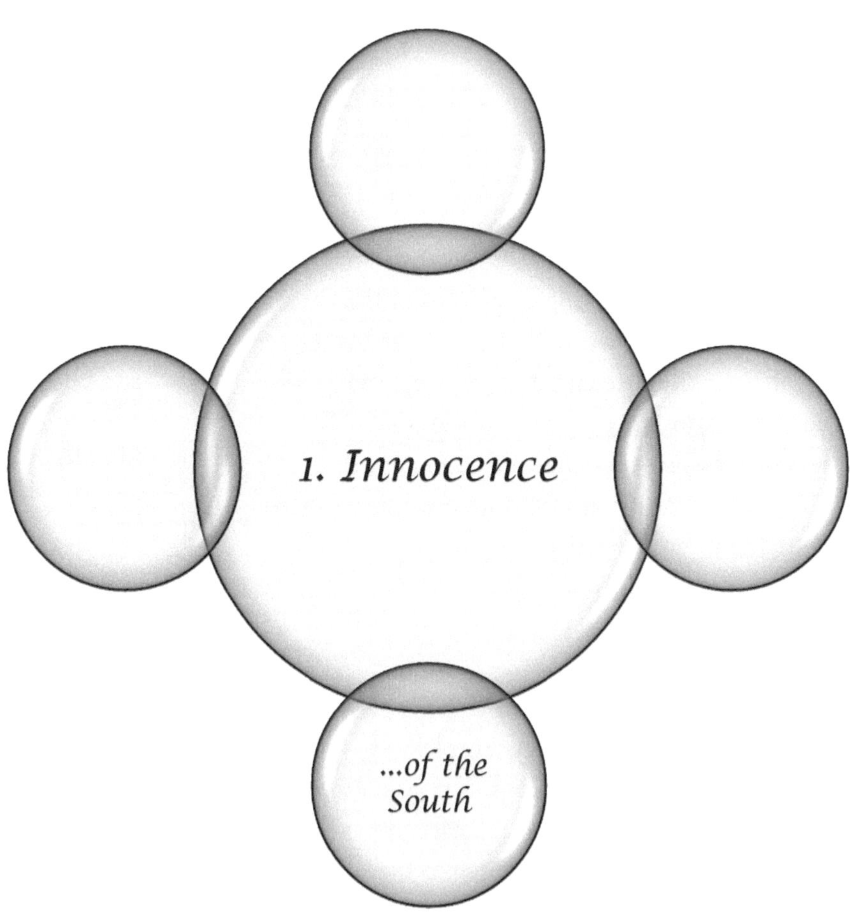

1. Innocence
...of the
South

OSTRAKA

Thou shalt remain, in midst of other woe
Than ours, a friend to man, to whom thou say'st
"Beauty is truth, truth beauty"—that is all
Ye know on earth, and all ye need to know.

> — "Ode on a Grecian Urn", John Keats

Apocalypses come and go, said the Pythian
at the end of her long shift as a voice of the
Oracle. Ends of the world happen every day
and for most they are a mercy, the depletion
of tedium, pain, ungrounded expectation. We
watched the departing chariots of Xerxes, slow
to vanish o'er the mountain horizon. His blood
had stirred by the prophecies of victory and
deafened him to whispers of a truer flow:
thou shalt remain in midst of other woe.

And so the Persian king of excess plowed
the forces of his nation through our land grown
dim by habit on the one hand, reason on the other,
and those who'd promised victory to the Greeks—
not us—were slain along with those who'd
prophecied defeat, but slipped away in haste
a handful of the keener minds did keep our sect alive.
Slender vessels through a night's high tide brought
wisdom to a rocky isle with glyphs and finer grist
than ours, a friend to man, to whom thou say'st,

Must we come around this way again?
I could not bear to answer thee,
for the tragedy at Delphi was our own,
the rupture caused by greater value placed
on quoting than of saying, the fear of disapproval
shutting veins and clarity, a ghostly pall
that had not lifted, so I stalled in hopes
that one of us would waken to that oldest
of the truths, I'm sure you can recall.
Beauty is truth, truth beauty—that is all.

So now we have our answer, friend. The cheerful
are still ostracized, potsherded for disloyalty
to cynical and grim. This earth is just beginning,
and if it comes to that, she's wise enough
to shake us off, throw out new continents, or
fashion greater sentience, above as now below.
Love and joy, like weather, have always created
conditions, and like the vapours of Delphi, your
sweet message to humanity will rise and show:
ye know on earth, and all ye need to know.

Note: The *ostraka* were potsherds used as ballots in the ancient Athenian practice of banishment, hence, the term we know today as "ostracism".

OH, HOW WE DANCED THROUGH THE EFFABLE!

—"Nurse's Song", William Blake

Blake fell off the shelf while I dusted, demanding
his turn at a glosa, poetic peeling back of a master's
quatrain to indulge this apprentice's decadence.
I set down my feathers and opened to the page.
But I've other things to write, William, and
could I add to your grain of sand renown
or frame o'erwise your Tyger burning bright?
No chance, said he, but in my fairest Albion
there is a dance where we may freely clown
then come home, my children, the sun is gone down.

Partnered with his mites and deviled angels,
I waltzed a quarter turn through ages.
Light of foot he was, this printer, illustrating
six thousand steps until my shoes spun off into
Jerusalem. I'm damned! Nay so, said he, pretend
to love and see—take interest and surprise
yourself by disapproving less. Our spirit
thunders while it lightens the oppressed—
be part! Let your choreography devise
and the dews of night arise.

Humble he was not, this man, wily dancer,
hand around my waist. I am no copier of
Nature but Imagination; expert you will see who
shades your rage more cleanly and more freely
than Rembrandt's light or Ruben with his curves,
for what is God's delighting but the Devil's finest play
in the gambling of our favours, in our orgiastic fright.
Watch Him raise your premonitions, cast them down
like ivory dice. Letting chips fall where they may,
come, come, leave off play, and let us away…

To the sweet quiet grove where a slow song
bids us hold our bodies close, our souls serene
wrapped breathless, while the hides and horns
of harsher life hold back awhile. Fear not, my
sweet, the bungle or the passing of the days;
no cause avoid but see it through your eyes
of Innocence wed true in Hell's tiled room to
Heaven. These grand balls are just beginning,
and a thousand years of joy will lift your sighs
till the morning appears in the skies.

VENTURING

Were the archangel, the dangerous one
Beyond the stars, to move down now
One step closer to us, we would die
From the fear in our own hearts.

—"The Second Elegy", Rainer Maria Rilke

All those blank spaces in my life
I kept from the historians;
all those years penned in captivity
I traveled halls whose doors
could not stay me
until the day my heart shredded from
tidings too harsh to bear;
walls closed in and the floor vanished
and a different voice intoned that you, undone,
were the archangel, the dangerous one.

Don't believe the chronicles
or if you must, note only the patterns
the seizures and deceits, disloyalties
and eschew the notion that humanity
has changed. It has not, cannot and won't!
You are not here to fix a broken plow
or elevate me to yet another throne;
I've had enough of velvet pillows
and food tasters. You and I must grow
beyond the stars, to move down now.

Beyond the fusty books, we share a backbone
radiant flow of here and now branching out
from my life to yours, from ours to all the others
like Indra's web, each life a pearl
fashioned by the sandy grit of thought,
but know this: the seeding of pain is not why
we are here nor to fill unread shelves
but to live true and full, erasing as we go
the lie, that should it come, bounteous supply,
one step closer to us, we would die.

The kingdoms we carved, I bequeath to you;
the vassals and the dungeons form a private terrain
where time and space meet as old friends
and complexities like muddy shoes are left at the door;
cut away the Gordian knot in your stomach,
make room for butterflies and fresh starts
catch the filaments of promise I throw to you;
together, let's pull ourselves to new heights,
giving thanks to Earth, freed, on recreated ramparts
from the fear in our own hearts.

Unbreaking Fine Threads: A Glosa

Not all our power is gone—not all our fame—
Not all the magic of our high renown—
Not all the wonder that encircles us—
Not all the mysteries that in us lie—

—"The Coliseum", Edgar Allan Poe

In dark pre-dawn I heard you creeping in—
no, I speak kind; you stumbled, crashing
the umbrella stand, that wedding gift unfit for
bumbershoots collapsed in spaceless entryways.
Old habit bade me leap: you freaking, no-good son—
but something stayed my hand and frame.
"Remain!" it spoke, a voice so firm I dared not
question, while fumes arose from me and
curled to ceiling height, a strange refrain:
not all our power is gone—not all our fame.

The kitchen light, the freezer door, then microwave;
how readable you are from this vast promontore
of stern and feckless view. I stay at home and
slap with angry trowel a sodden clay to cracks
of this relationship that crumbles from a dearth
of moisturing; my fierce determined frown
to harridan it leads where once I'd been
your sugarbean and you my peppercorn,
we've shredded our affinity to clown.
Not all the magic of our high renown

22

Can bridge the damage of your faithless
roving eye—did I not try to fill your lonely
crevices of expectation? "Refrain!" What?
The voice again comes scolding me as if
the steps ascending to this crumpled bed
were innocent, and I thrill-seeking devious.
Whose side, I shout, take you, oh fiend, oh
patron saint of treachery? Say what, you slur
and stare as if a horror were now obvious,
not all the wonder that encircles us.

You fall upon the feral bed we shared
until the one who gave you voice appeared
and gifts we thought were provident divided
us. Cleave not, the priest in Fiji said, ambiguous,
before we walked a bed of coals, mad newlyweds.
Fare well. It is, I see, no worthy sacrifice to die
for life it is that reconciles and ties the tiny
threads of love in capillary flow. The clot that
stopped my heart and brain will ne'er belie
not all the mysteries that in us lie.

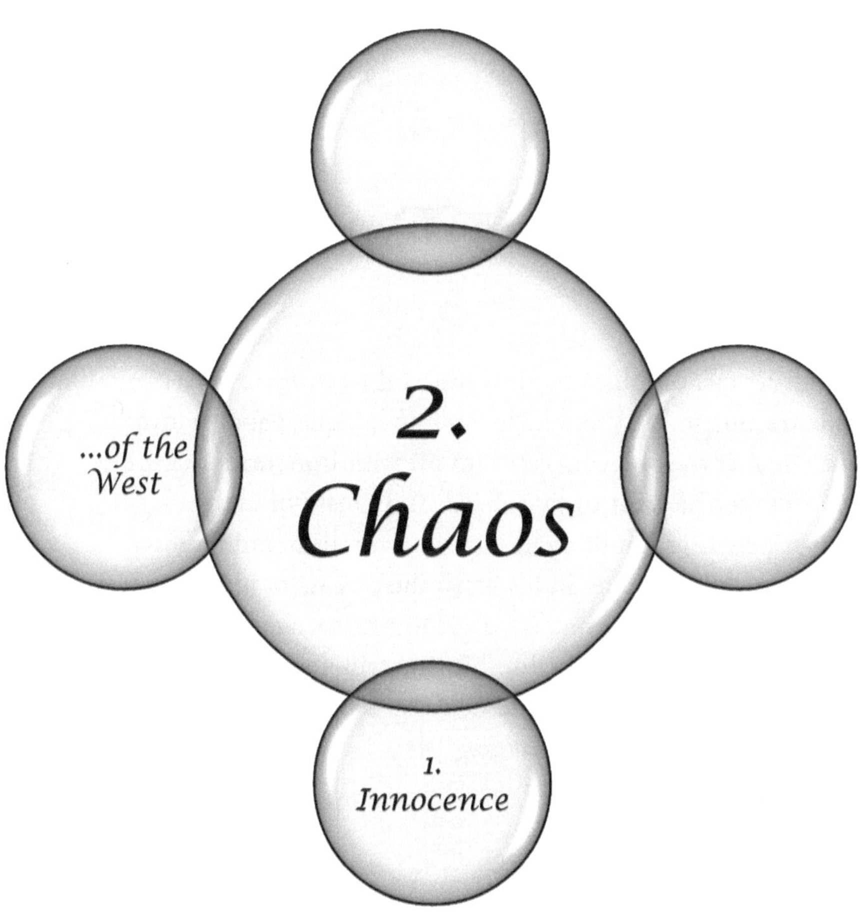

...of the West
2.
Chaos
1.
Innocence

THE TWISTED CREW OF S.S. DISAPPOINTMENT

If I be a diviner, full of the divining spirit that wanders on high mountain
  ridges
between two seas, wandering between the past and future like a heavy
  cloud—
hostile to sultry plains, to all that is weary, that can neither die nor live:
ready for lightning in its dark bosom, and for the redeeming flash of light.

—Thus Spake Zarathustra, Friedrich Nietzsche

This is no tale of mine, and if it were I'd lie to spare myself and him
embarrassment. He was a lucky man in conquest and in love
until he met the one who cast him off with iron heart and subtle twirl,
and so to sea he went to shovel coal and dream of oversouls
and shapely hips, thinking he was born for great and mighty
missions while slapping in his berth the tiny nasty biting midges.
One night on deck he met a mate, long-haired and shadowy, who
offered him a smoke and said, this ship will never let you off, you'll not
see land except as memory and ne'er again view life from golden bridges
if I be a diviner, full of the divining spirit that wanders on high mountain
  ridges.

For years they drifted and the crew they never stayed the same,
only the man retained his weighty shapes and disbeliefs, a cold and
lonely core he held against the world—you do not understand!—
became his cage, the coal he shoveled gave no heat. The captain
raged, I'll hold your pay, reduce your daily rations to rank water,
weeviled biscuits lest you cease to pander to the deadened crowd
your hauntings and disharmonies—you lost at love, big deal!—this
recollecting will not feed the furnace of a ship nor soul, and those you
call your friends, you fool, they'll blow no soothing breeze, only a
    shroud
between two seas, wandering between the past and future like a heavy
    cloud.

Deeper into gloom and poverty the sailor, rose to captain,
sank while gathered from himself a crew of grim impediment
who kept him safe from sentiment, the softness of a spirit
he once knew and was, no longer traceable upon his face;
his bones and sinews twisted, height he lost, his guts
no longer moved, a constipate, the power to forgive
himself star-crossed and so he sailed on restless never-
ending seas and shoveled coal that blackened what remained of
true and freshing thought—he tried but could not find a way to give,
hostile to sultry plains, to all that is weary, that can neither die nor live.

They came upon his ship one summer eve
along the Baltic coast, he'd drifted further north
than he had ever known, a tropic soul no longer
owned by lover, wife or kin, he came aboard
and boasted of the liberty he'd sown, no boundaries
or chains; he could not see the loathsome fright
the suit of iron links he wore connecting him
to every debt and disappointment, crossing times and
space, entangled, at its core, a grotesque, squirming sprite
ready for lightning in its dark bosom, and for the redeeming flash of light.

PLEASERS

> *Faith and unfaith can ne'er be equal powers;*
> *Unfaith in aught is want of faith in all.*
> *It is the little rift within the lute*
> *That by and by will make the music mute.*

—*Idylls of the King*, Alfred, Lord Tennyson

Here lies Edimora Jones of fragile bones
in the plushest bed she's known since
Al Capone fired off his Valentines, and she
and Kenny honeymooned in Sioux Lookout
then moved to Saskatoon. Poor thing worked
herself to death, pre-ordered her own flowers
so others wouldn't have to. Forevermore, she's
doomed to lie with Kenny here who screwed and
drank his way to Shady Lane's spring showers.
Faith and unfaith can ne'er be equal powers.

My name is Merlin, and I run this grave. A quiet
job, there's not much call for wizarding in death;
of spells and faithless queens I've had enough,
and lust will find its way through any means. But
you, I see, have come for different cause: you've
taken up your sword and slayed the Hydra, squall
of whipper-snapping, salivating heads, all slavering
for tastes of younger-than, deserve-I-do, and other
sweet entitlements. Over-think and then they fall.
Unfaith in aught is want of faith in all.

Pleasers come in every shape and size, the
handsome ones, once loved, they yearn to hear
again the sighs—which they'll deny—whilst chasing
pretty foals who only wish to graze in peace; and
those whom beauty never marked, they'll scrub
the ark for but a glance, a touch, though be it brute.
Heed well toward whom you praise and why, there
is no sky lofts higher than your own, no time you're
bound to give away, unless it's freely tendered fruit.
It is the little rift within the lute

That plays a sour tune, a tinny thievish lonely
rhapsody, that desecrates the lungs and breaks
the heart without accompanying joy. Do not deploy
such measures in your mortal ache for pleasure.
You are God's ultimate, His timely good—provide
no servitude to lazies and to miscreants. Shoot,
look at you! Your deft and fine design, your playful
mind, your suppleness, have faith in these!
Ignore the sinuosity of gravity, so sad, irresolute
that by and by will make the music mute.

SIEGE

There are certain things I will not tell you
you will find your way among the roses I write
because certain redundancies are not given to silence
or the sorrows of the soul, or the pleasures of the body.

      —"Certain Things are Priceless", Gavriel Navarro

Our bus broke down last night on the outskirts
of Montségur, that castled sugar loaf where dualists
held out until the last of them was set to flame and
choice of thought once more was laid aside in favour
of the true. I would have texted you had it not been
for the shepherd who assisted us; a Basque, he drew
me to his mountain heights, we left the others with
their bedrolls and their blogs, we hardly spoke, his
grin was slow and shy, and very soon I knew
there are certain things I will not tell you.

I can say this: the sheep that break the fences
of the prohibitions that protect a sense of dignity
that's false are God's true creatures, and the others?
Well, we've all been fleeced and sold for meat and
cheese; I cannot count myself as rebel when it suits
me, nor is the reflex jolt of recognition proof of right
or wrong or better. Yet I must speak of disappointment
as I see it, every time the falling short becoming more
predictable, so you'll pardon me, I hope, this flight;
you will find your way among the roses that I write.

And when the space between your words and mine
dissolves and fades to dim, I will not plow you under
nor make of you a gilt-edged memory to swap with
buddies at the lonely-hearted food court. Our life spans
were extended for much more than this, and so I'll
take my sandwiches and canvas sack of impudence
in search of signs that say don't touch, abandoned
mines and circling, pointless stairs. No more a fitful
subjugate, I happily discard the weight of our events
because certain redundancies are not given to silence

And this was never meant to be a sorry tale. That's what
we were making, you and I—endurance and longevity
as ends are bleeding bores—so celebrate we should that
in the nick of time, the Peugot on the hairpin road becomes
instead an accident to fling us from the factual, contractual,
and when I take that shepherd's hand, I'll turn to free
you from your wreckage. The dusty road to Compostelle
has many cul-de-sacs not on the map; it doesn't mean
we're lost. The siege is done. We never gave up liberty
or the sorrows of the soul, or the pleasures of the body…

THE MINDS THAT I HAVE LOVED

The sort of beauty that I have approved
prosper but little, has dried up of late,
yet knows that to be choked with hate,
may well be of all evil chances chief.

—"A Prayer for My Daughter", William Butler Yeats

They will say of us, perhaps, it had to be,
this gathering of poets, our politic of rivalries
and odd compressed complexities. The Faerie
Queen, she warned us of photonic cluster
fucks, while you have trouble yet, I see,
accepting her reality, yet she has moved
more mountains than Mohammed with her
smooth eventuality. I'm busy now with tasks
of shrugging off used baggage to improve
the sort of beauty that I have approved.

My reason-addled mind forewarns I haven't
read enough of Yeats to merit this pretension,
but consort of the famous Mab, who deals in
space, not time, insists the day I gazed upon
the Book of Kells I was by Dublin given
sacrament and Irish has a nature potentate—
that meeting with St. Paul, the drubbing
had their place. Unfolding store of starchy
arguments by laundresses whose weight
prosper but little, has dried up of late.

And so the cities gather on the tracts of
inner lands where peace has come to reign:
Lisbon brings Pessoa, Baltimore the tracks
of Poe, it is these minds of wanderers I love
and those who ply their trade upon my rivers
of contentment. I see him in the congregate,
my lover at this terminus of not-quite flesh
and shady bone, no poet he but understands
this magic and our artistry as consummate
yet knows that to be choked with hate

would only complicate our tendencies toward
treachery. Steep lessons learned, the curves
of bell, do they apply? Who knows? We live
a paisley life, we die, then live again sometimes
within a moment's space. You leave a trace
of bread crumbs, winding threads, motif
of mystery and myth, no waste. Our minds
will find a rhythm of their own, we'll throw
into the world a posit which we hold that grief
may well be of all evil chances chief.

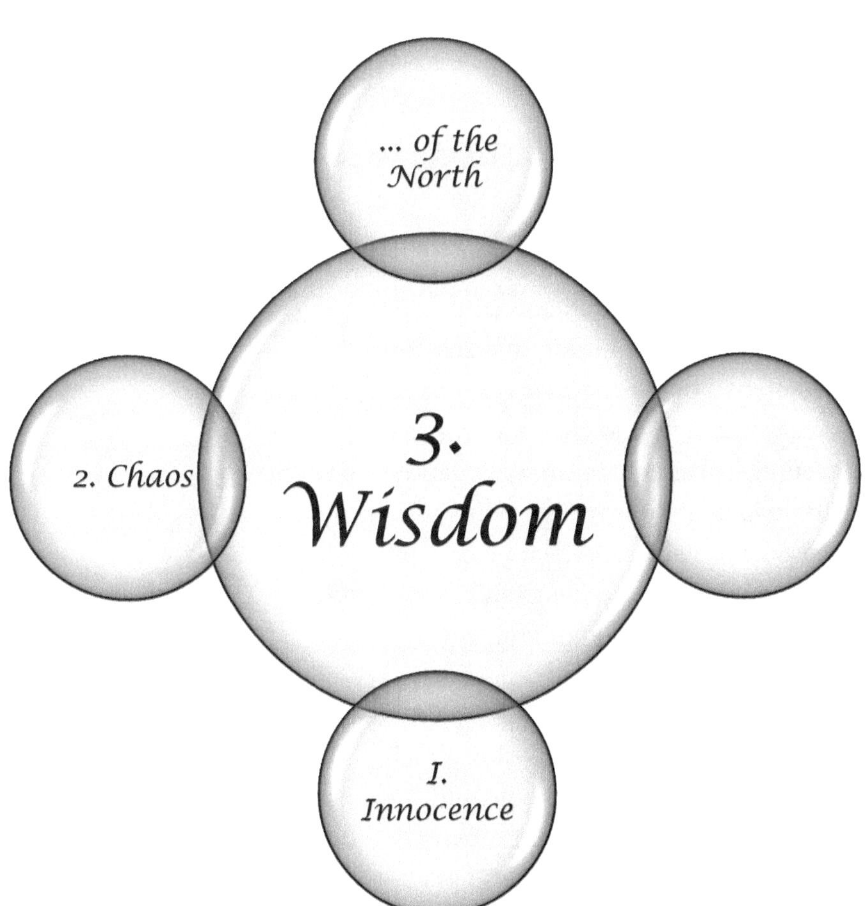

... of the North
2. Chaos
3.
Wisdom
1.
Innocence

A BRANCH OF FAMILY TREE I SAW: A GLOSA

Philosophers in vain so long have sought;
In vain, though by their powerful art they bind
Volatile Hermes, and call up unbound
In various shapes, old Proteus from the sea.

—Paradise Lost, Book III, John Milton

Steadying myself through excess of Brontë
and harsher tales of moor and cliff, I spy
at last the strains of Puritan that strain the
blood of my good kin. Resolve I thus to cut away
what serves me not, to clear the woods of all
that sunlight cannot warm; what darkness brought
I can no longer effulgate, these limits sicken,
viral knots post-Gordian, who cares? Sow
peace, your hospitals and prison guards cannot,
philosophers in vain so long have sought.

Oh, dreary flock led by the unimagined,
when did thy curious and noble minds depart,
that you would now sit 'mongst pews so bleak
and apostolic that no news from paradise
will ever reach your ears, convinced you are
by dullards' bleats of scripture rendered blind
in search of sin and hate—lo, found, abominate!
Succinct, so easy to relate. Plod home then,
dig deep 'neath cushions, click remotes to find
in vain, though by their powerful art they bind.

My blood and bones hold vibrancy, and so
do yours! Before the nailing of the Treatises
that Luther swore, we were the Catholic, true
and only church and prior were the pagans,
country folk adhered to Nature's rise and fall,
bipolar swings equate mad reasonings surround
us with the fears of ages cleft for me in rocks
and stormy hymns, no hers but bonneted and prim,
I trim these branches merciless, willing to confound
volatile Hermes, and call up unbound

rich and manifold the Paradise surrounding us
I sacrifice the sting of death to live this life
already deemed eternal, for where's the sense in
waiting till we have no arms or voice to dance
and sing? Rebirth is slow and tedious, a grinding
wheel when wings would serve more prettily
we fly, we soar when images of harmony supplant
the previous, no longer worded or recalled, and
scoop with lustred scallop shells, we free
in various shapes, old Proteus from the sea.

FREEDOM IS NOT THE ABSENCE OF SLAVERY: A GLOSA

Boast not of advantages that belong to another.
Creation tolerates a horse that whinnies, "I am beautiful"
But repudiates the one who brags: "I own a beautiful horse."
Your truest advantage? The uses you make of your imagination.

—*The Handbook*, Epictetus

On a day the words wouldn't come, when nothing lay before me
but tasks and impediments, I was certain, to the freedom of
creation, I hauled my world-weary self across town, hands
wrapped around a double shot espresso, to call on my friend
who breaks the necks of chickens and lambs behind the
St. Lawrence Market. *C-r-r-r-ack!* Hey, how ya been, brother?
His grin made spacious by brawls in stalls and ports of call
where trafficking in human flesh goes on and where he'd
carved with tainted ink the last true words from his mother,
Boast not of advantages that belong to another,

before they broke his legs and threw him on a ship because
he was young and pretty and had eyelashes like a mountain
pony. He's not even sure of his name. They'll remember me,
he likes to say, as Slave, though it sounds fancier in Balkan.
A slave owns nothing but his own possibility for happiness.
But what about freedom, I used to argue. Is it just a mouthful
of letters too cheap to die for? Go ahead, ask him that one—
he'll look you in the eye so deep, you'll think he dug to China.
Claim that you have rights, and he'll sock you an earful:
Creation tolerates a horse that whinnies, "I am beautiful,"

38

but who the hell grants you these so-called rights? Think that
way, you're already in chains! He thanks me for the double shot,
beefy arms sticky with blood and feathers, and accompanied
by the hushed cluck of hens amenable to fate, hears me
out. We sit on overturned buckets. Whatever you are, you are,
he says. Hungry, thirsty, selfish, live with it! They're prime course,
ticket to your second favourite F-word. Walk through a mall, any
city in the world, don't count the slaves, listen how absence yearns
for freemen whose nose rings aren't pulled by smart phone force
but repudiates the one who brags, "I own a beautiful horse."

Absence yearns. That's how you know it's working, says the old
stoic. Those slaves you see, clicking and liking and scrolling and
texting, are driven by it too—we all are—but they don't know they've
been bought and sold, and the market's never gonna set them free.
But what about?—he won't let me finish. Worst thing you can do
is chase your thoughts. The good ones, let 'em come. Ingratiation
to that mad driver in your head or to anyone who tries to fool you into
trading joy for guilt and sadness, that's the first link in the chain.
Ride your own carriage. Guaranteed, it'll take you to the right station.
Your truest advantage? The uses you make of your imagination.

THE HAUNTED YARD SALE: A GLOSA

Be a falcon in your effort, be a tiger in your strength
Be an expert in hunting, be brave in war
Don't hang around with the peacock and the nightingale
One's conceited, the other talks too much.

—A Rubai by Rumi, translation by Nevit O. Ergin

We followed the signs down County Seventeen:
Massive moving sale, everything must go. I am
no fan of other people's treasures, I barely love
my own, but it's worth the pleasure of seeing you
relaxed and so I navigate, pointing out balloons
tied to fence posts and yield signs. The length
of you in the driver's seat, arm outside the window,
turns my head—Look there! I shout. A red barn
rises where there'd been only corn. The poet singeth
Be a falcon in your effort, be a tiger in your strength.

Who said that? You've walked on ahead, as usual,
and do not hear my question. You seem inebriated by
the signs—Everything, and we mean EVERYTHING,
must go!!! Ours is the only car on the arrow-straight
dirt driveway on a sunny Saturday morn, what's
up with that? The barn, as we draw closer, is enor-
gigantimous, a made-up word I know you hate, and
there's a gleaming John Deere tractor parked beside
a flawless leafy crop. Something wicked is in store.
Be an expert in hunting, be brave in war.

What war? The doors to the big red barn are open;
they draw you in like plankton to a whale. I follow.
Not a soul is in the space that's crammed from floor
to lofty beam with chinoiserie and wicker, with mouse-
chewed magazines, *Life* and *Time,* with Churchill
and Hiroshima, post-mushroom, covers that regale
conflicts that predate us. Remember naught but
pleasures and blessings, says a turbaned figure pale.
Don't hang around with the peacock and the nightingale.

Gripping density of battle-thought is the evilest of sin,
and then he whirled, counterclockwise. You must spin
it all away, he said, and rise to brighter, lighter climes
if paradise you seek, then paradise you'll surely find.
What could be simpler? Hey, look at this, you cry from
behind the whirling dervish. Have you ever seen such
artistry? I glance from ghostly spinning host to you and
calculate our difference. A beringed transparent palm
extends to take your twenty for a broken, lime green crutch.
One's conceited, the other talks too much.

WHO RIDES THE WEST WIND

AN ACROSTIC GLOSA

He who waits on his god has a protecting angel
The humble man who fears his goddess accumulates wealth;
My friend, your mind is a river whose spring never fails,
The accumulated mass of the sea, which knows no decrease.

—"The Babylonian Theodicy", an acrostic poem by
Saggil-kīnam-ubbib, translation by W. G. Lambert

Nimrod was a hunter. He never wanted to be king.
Excuse me? That'll be $14.33, said the spotty kid
With the squeegee. Wan' me to check your oil?
Whatever I thought he'd said had shot its way
Into the back rafters of my neural networks like a
Nesting swallow. Oil's good. I paid and drove off through a
Deluge of pea-sized hail into a weird greening twillight to
Seven Sisters, a snug gabled inn at the base of Sloane valley.
Squash soup alone beneath a faded cross-stitch, dated 1797:
He who waits on his god has a protecting angel.

Oversight, that lower case g—had to be, I thought,
Winding down later with brandy in hot springs outside my room.
That night, I woke up, not alone. He sat in the armchair,
Hair to his shoulders, bare chested, linen kilt falling open—
And a manly view. *Hello.* I threw the spare pillow at him and he
Tossed it back. Who the fu—he lifted his hand and all my
Inner clamour vanished. You're getting better, he said,
At inner silence. Eventually, I stammered: Are—are you
My angel? No, I am your god, as I'm sure you've heard
The humble man who fears his goddess accumulates wealth.

How…who? Nimrod. His eyes crinkled in greeting, and he
Extended an arm to help peel me from the headboard.
Personal gods have fallen out of fashion, but we've never
Retreated or abandoned our posts. I sat, stupified
On the edge of the bed. What are you doing here at
My getaway weekend? He smiled. You invited me.
I'm here at your life and at your service. He called me
Something that sounded like—no, no, not doofus, he
Explained. You're like a goofah, spinning without oars, but
My friend, your mind is a river whose spring never fails

Even in the dry spells, and my currents have always
Sustained you. Goofah—round reed boat in Akkadian or
Sumerian, as I recalled. So, do you need a fatted lamb?
Am I supposed to worship you? God no, he laughed. Personal
Gods are friends, known from many pasts. My job is to deliver
Exactly what you ask for, in proportions cooperatively designed to
Raise your expectations and add to them. At multiplication, I am
Expert. No kidding! I have been crazy happy lately. Is that your work?
Sure, and we are just beginning. Soon your happiness will match
The accumulated mass of the sea, which knows no decrease.

Note: "The Babylonian Theodicy" is the world's oldest preserved acrostic poem, written in Sumerian and dating to approximately 1700 BCE. Acrostic refers to a hidden message contained in a specific ordering of letters, most commonly the first letter in each line, read downward.

The full theodicy contained 27 stanzas of 11 lines each and featured a dialogue between a sufferer and his friend. Many of the lines have disintegrated, but the acrostic is still readable and translates roughly as: "I, Saggil-kīnam-ubbib, the incantation priest, am adorant of the god and the king."

The deciphering of this acrostic glosa is left to the reader, and the poet chose to ignore the traditional rhyme scheme to shift emphasis.

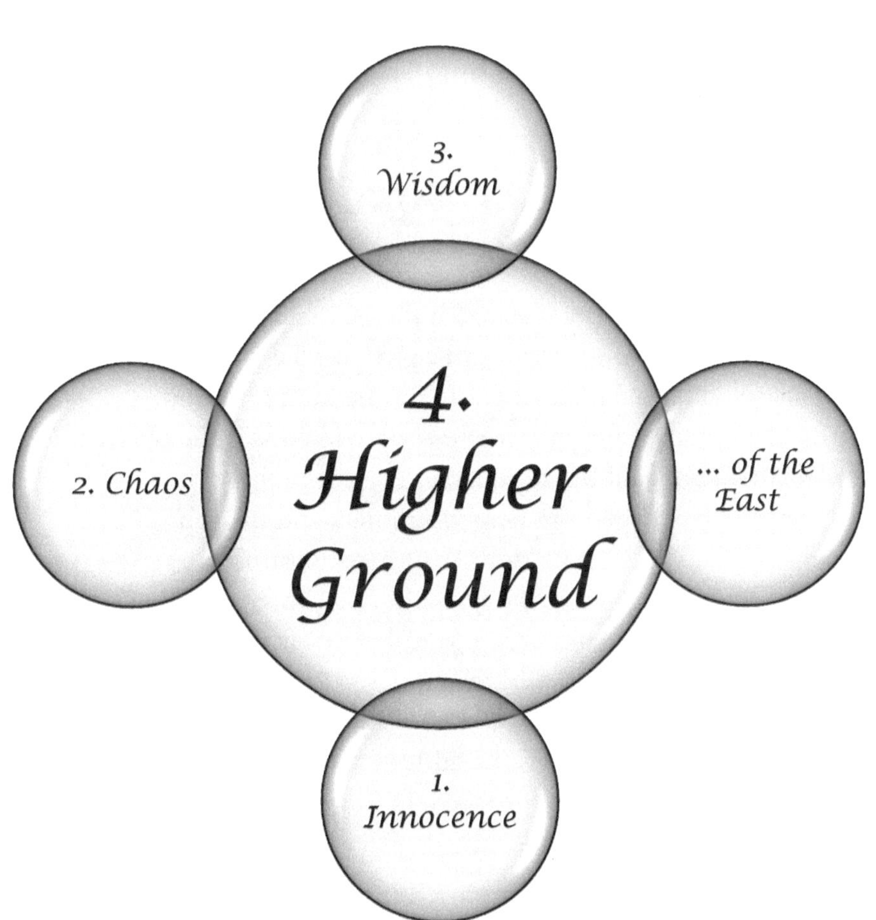

3.
Wisdom
4.
Higher
Ground
2. Chaos
... of the
East
1.
Innocence

THE QUIVER OF INANNA

What she has crushed to powder never will rise up
The scent of fear stains her robe, she wears
The carved-out ground plan of heaven and earth, who seeks
Her word does not look to An, the great god assembly.

—"Lady of the Largest Heart", Enheduanna, translation
by Diane Wolkstein

The gray-bearded merchant stared at the bills and coins
I had placed in his hand. Sorry, did I give you the wrong
currency? You have the method, not yet the means, he said,
setting down the money. My friend and I had crossed the river
Jordan after dark, and the antiquarian shop could have fit in
Jerusalem or Barcelona. We were in Amman, and the cup
of lapis-studded silver was a steal. Wait here. Returning
from the back room: forget the soap dish, take this
and, *maktub*, on dates and honey, you shall freely sup.
What she has crushed to powder never will rise up.

The leather pouch, length and breadth of my forearm, one
cubit, had been patched and stitched in so many places,
I wondered if the original still existed. You are holding it,
he said. Hmm…what? I mused. The quiver of Inanna.
Lightning jolts ran up both arms, exploded in my chest
while down below, something volatile shot spears
both east and west. The Sufi nodded as if I'd passed
some kind of test. Inanna means By Way of Now, she is
the space within the quiver, downward motion of your tears;
the scent of fear stains her robe, she wears.

Did this once hold arrows? The sharpest, he replied,
fashioned by the hunter who became the king of the
city of eternal increase. Nimrod! Personal god, I
thought in a small, shy way, but why? One of each,
male and female, our capacitors, they bring by presence
and design non-substance to firmament. Weeks
ago, I'd walked and talked with the god of my being.
How could it be sacrilege to hold the nature of
my own goddess? We are both. In anima she speaks
the carved-out ground plan of heaven and earth, who seeks.

You said I have the method. What are the means?
Attraction, he said, wrapping the cup. Aversion. Honouring
both, receiving and expelling. In Bab-El, such adepts
were called the overturned, man become woman,
woman, man. Genesis understates. The city of increase
thrived for millenia of millenia, and this you can see
through the windows of your mitochondria, tiny arks that
survived the deluge that balanced drought, the doubting
sin. Logos, singular spirit of Word, lives forever free;
Her word does not look to An, the great god assembly.

IP STANDS FOR ICE POINT, DON'T YOU KNOW?

If to be welcomed by the good, O Book! thou make thy steady aim
No empty chatterer will dare to question or dispute thy claim.
But if perchance thou hast a mind to win of idiots' approbation,
Lost labour will be thy reward, though they'll pretend appreciation.

— Miguel de Cervantes, commendatory verse by Urganda the
Unknown to *Don Quixote de la Mancha*

I'd been dreaming an impossible dream of my nights on Broadway. I'm not
the actor, you are, but the leader of the workshop on the cruise ship had been
adamant—see huge your crowds, with fervour tell the story of your glory,
leaning always toward the feeling in the moment of relief. All this folderol
of copyrights and wrongs, of intellectual properties (IPs) had frozen me
like peas, so instead of novels I wrote jingles for potato chips, a decent game,
they paid me well, I could maintain the sense that life had turned out not
so bad, and happiness was mine as long as I took water, not red wine, with
my little yellow pills. And then that morning, from the bathroom drain:
If to be welcomed by the good, O Book! Thou make thy steady aim—

The good? Excuse me? I turned my toothbrush off; the mirror was still
clouded from the shower, and the image, pinkish-red, was me, all right,
no genies—Cervantes felt the same, hemmed in by rank authorities,
imprisoned for indebtedness, not unlike your mortgage—I spun around to
find a stranger in green tights, exhorting. I probably would have fainted if
I weren't such a groupie. Aren't you that Canadian? I forget your name.
Robert Goulet. Kiley would have come, he loved the role, but he's in
Ipswich guiding Chaucer through a knotty tale. Don't worry, you're only
naked in my mind—all women were. I've come to bring you fame.
No empty chatterer will dare to question or dispute thy claim.

My teeth were chattering; he handed me my robe. You didn't talk
all 'thee' and 'thy' in life, I said. Why now? My mother'd loved his eyes,
I could see why. I'm practicing, he said, for future roles, I'll only win
if you can be persuaded to abandon your potato crisps…chips, he edited,
with winning smile. Poor Guinevere, I thought—with Goulet playing
Lancelot, she didn't stand a chance. But 'neath the lurid excitation
I was nothing but confused. I can explain, he said. In days of knights
errant and ladies fair, there moved a force mysterious who guaranteed
safe passage through litigious, superstitious and societal vexation,
but if perchance thou hast a mind to win of idiots' approbation,

which I don't think you do, you're made of sterner stuff—but once
the guardian has made her wishes known, as she did to Cervantes while
he languished in his prison, then it's best you drop your fears of false
authority and take up what you've come here to achieve. The lyricists
await—did you know the poet Auden wrote La Mancha's early songs?
But they were scrapped for cutting to the bone too close, agitation
of the masses wasn't welcomed like today . . . the prophecies Goulet
dispensed came true. *Olé!* Within a year, I dropped the chips, I wrote a
book and sold it to a playwright for big bucks, never minding the sensation:
Lost labour will be thy reward, though they'll pretend appreciation.

Note: "Man of La Mancha" was a Broadway musical that opened in
1965, lyrics by Joe Darion, music by Mitch Leigh. The play was
based on a book by Dale Wasserman who'd been inspired by
Cervantes's 17th century masterpiece. Richard Kiley (1922-1999)
played the original Broadway role of Cervantes/Quixote. Robert
Goulet (1933-2007) played the lead in the 1997-98 US national tour.

POTS AND POETRY

O wrangling schools, that search what fire
Shall burn this world, had none the wit
Unto this knowledge to aspire
That this her fever might be it?

—"A Fever", John Donne

Of a Tuesday, I set out to take the air, slipping
through the trade door nearest to the scuttle,
having heard enough of dukes and their whineries
to last a month of war days, when who,
upon the wooded road should call my name but you,
clanking and bejangling, your tattered cloak a dire
recall to me that once you'd been a friend and more,
while now you travel door to door, or so I'd heard.
I pause and then with anger some, inquire,
O wrangling schools that search, what fire

hast brought thee to this new demise
of mending tin when once you were our brightest?
The sheepish face, your downcast eyes
arouse me to a higher sense and when amidst
the soldered pots I spy a book of verse
my knees grow weak and so I pull you, kindred spirit,
to the oak where once we read and rhymed sublime,
where disciplined and learning warmly gatheréd;
but you, dear muse, none else, I must admit
shall burn this world, had none the wit.

The lady whom we shall not name has cast me
from her bed, you said, and with her ban saw fit
to bolt the school, and that is not the worst of it.
My books of rhyme upon a pyre, and our good
name made laughingstock for loyalties misplaced.
My flesh takes in your soft iambs while sadness and
a host of anguishes sweep through me, kindling fire.
To wound a poet of your rank, I say, is heinous
while poetic minds crowd here and so admire
unto this knowledge to aspire.

The air around you brightens. Have you need of pots
and poems then? I've trod a verse and two these years,
blown airy sonnets through a bellows, extolled the triolet;
the tinker's craft leaves space for lowly mind and ear
to fabricate—you pause. My hands, now ringed and
lanolined, they were not always thus. To be done, poet,
with the past, I'd celebrate, and our talent has not grown
beyond our need of you. Nor has mine, think I, an outcry to
your ear, while mine hears you. One small kiss to win her spirit,
that this her fever might be it?

REVIVING THE BLUE BALLOON

But go on, Ishmael, said I at last; don't you hear?
Get away from before the door; your patched boots
are stopping the way. So on I went. I now by instinct
followed the streets that took me waterward.

—*Moby Dick*, Herman Melville

He was one of my best customers and
his name is not Ishmael, though he was the
son of a handmaid, and my inn, The Blue
Balloon, lies three blocks from the docks
of New Bedford, so you can call me anything
but hey, Gar! I answer readily to, "Cold beer,
ya got some?" Two centuries ago, I might have
been a whaler, while Ish, he sought finer ways
to whelm Leviathan, purveyor of our measly fear.
But go on, Ishmael, said I at last, don't you hear?

He did, and so he built a blue balloon from scratch
with Neoprene and plans from the brothers
Montgolfier. In no time, he grew rich from rides
above Atlantic tides, while me and my saloon
became a B & B for clammy folk who trade inside
and swallow gormless fish like me. Our sweet cahoots
grew checkered like the skin of old Queequeg. Serving
whine and ail, I knew no happy hours except from 3-5,
hand-stirring bellinis and martinis with exotic fruits.
Get away from before the door, your patched boots

do not belong, I yelled that stormy night at Ish
who'd spent the day Nantucket-way with dolphins
and young whales escorting him to thermal heights.
I hate my life, this bust balloon! I yanked great wads
of cash from out the till while Ishmael calmly took
a mop to spills and said, you're on the brink
of doing what you came to do as I already am—
I snapped. Are you my guru now? Scant chance
have I to fly while bottom-feeding corporate skinks
are stopping the way. So on I went. I now by instinct

wailed the jargon of poor, rich pitiable me, and
Ishmael, he just let me exercise my blowhole—
a waste, I know, of good cetology! And when I'd blown
my furies out, I stopped, while thunderbolts and hail
lashed on, ice pellets at the window laughing at
the Ahab I'd become, a one-track Captain Nerd
pursuing a great white that bit and swallowed and
expectorated me. Clear skies tomorrow, Ishmael smiled.
You ready to fly? Oh, aye! Yes, I, fledgling thunderbird,
followed the streets that took me waterward.

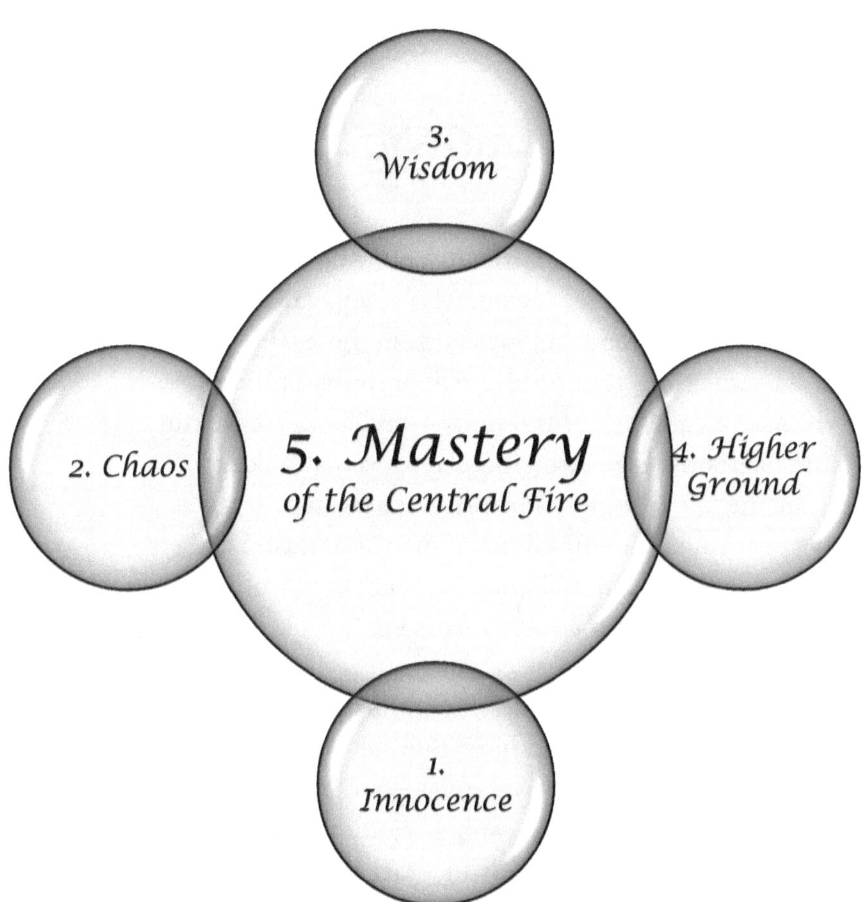

3.
Wisdom
2. Chaos
5. Mastery
of the Central Fire
4. Higher
Ground
1.
Innocence

MEETING AT THE BRIDGE OF QUINAMETZIN

I know that I have lived because I have felt
and, feeling giving me the knowledge of my existence,
I know likewise that I shall exist no more
when I shall have ceased to feel.

—*The Memoirs*, Giacomo Casanova

We have been awaiting you, friend. You, whose luck
and patience have run out—you, who've squeezed
the final drops of blood and loyalty from those who
suck the same from you. All this talk of rivers running
to the sea, of equilibrium and unity—my, look, you've run
yourself aground! The cards you played, you also dealt;
they are the fate that growls before you now, four-legged
surly apparition, bridging courts of man and beast. I am
Coyote, keeper of distorted knowing, backward truth, unspelt.
I know that I have lived because I have felt.

When parcels of you run away, my brothers and my sisters
watch them sink, recede and hide; they never leave your
shores, the lies, the broken lives, they fester. Surrounding
you, we hunt—hyena, jackal, wolf—we are the strategists,
we trap, press in, we corner, leaving space enough that
you feel safe, content again with mere subsistence
tearing at the flesh, denied or glutted, all the same, not
satisfied, until the shadows you've decried arrive, well
dressed and boast, Behold, my wobble-free resistance
and feeling giving me the knowledge of my existence.

And now you see this bridge is wide enough for only
one. Behind me lies the kingdom you believe awaits you
with the sweetling fruits and ecstasies your earthly courts
cannot provide. By me and my compatriots, you shall
not pass, I am the trickful god, and if you turn, you'll see
the bridge behind you is no more. You've burnt the score
you kept with every give and take; withholding—you were
right—it costs the most. The hoardings of affection make
of me a phantom, crawled upon your slippery shore;
I know likewise that I shall exist no more.

But this I would not seek if I were you, now standing
with one foot on awkward ground, the other hovering
uncertain of the step—you've claimed so many, have
you not? With every choice, a million die, and who am
I to tell you every road not taken thrives? So keen are
you to die and birth again, in painful strips you peel
the memories of cretin, hero, villain you have played. So
here's the deal: Cross you may when you can hold your
gaze while I, through slow dismemberment reveal
when I shall have ceased to feel.

Note: Quinametzin are a race of giants, believed in Nahuatl
(Aztec/Maya) mythology to have designed and built the pyramids of
Teotihuacan, Mexico. Dismemberment, which eventually degraded
to human sacrifice by the Aztecs, was a shamanistic discipline
referring to acknowledgement, ownership and affection toward one's
shadow self and the shadow of others. This life-long endeavour was
also known as the Backward Facing Path with Coyote, trickster god,
functioning as guide.

BEYONDING BUDDHA: THE WORLD'S GREATEST LOVER

Whether I shall turn out to be the hero of my own life, or whether
that station will be held by anybody else, these pages must show.
To begin my life with the beginning of my life, I record that I
Was born (as I have been informed and believe) on a Friday.

—David Copperfield, Charles Dickens

An Englishman named Oliver lives above a fado bar on a back street
in the Algarve—perhaps you've heard, he was renowned back in
the day as the world's greatest lover. Filed them he did by country
and ability to please. How he fell to keeper of blues Portuguese
depends less upon which lover you ask than the state of your own
expectations. Mine were seldom great and so I spoke to him of weather
over ruby port and stilton, and watched him place his hand near mine
and turn his chair to face the beach, to cast a sheen upon his wavy
copper hair. I ate some cheese and then declared, I'll tolerate no tether,
whether I shall turn out to be the hero of my own life, or whether

you believe you have some canny skill to turn my vast indifference
to thrill. He held his pose, though from the side he peered, examining
my gaze and mien. You're from the East, he cried. I am, practitioner
of Yin, said I, well trained by—monks, I nearly said, allowing him to
think the thought instead. He twisted in his seat, I've learned a thing
or two myself of secrets that do tantalize. You'll tell me what you know?
Of course. I offered my best smile, mirror bright, if you'll agree to share
your history. The prophets have aligned in higher realms, pulled back
to raise our own divinity. I seek awakened bodies, yours or not, if so,
that station will be held by anybody else, these pages must show.

I've interviewed them all—the sluts, lotharios, God's greatest gifts
they're not! Attention-seeking, loneliness, the craving to be owned,
these are the devil's twist, their pleasures brief and framed with
painful entropy. The world's true lovers must be free, if they be
counted great in Heaven's shining panoply. A single night, a passing
glance, the power to intoxicate and kindle fire eternal in the eye,
these are the human rights and skills that modesty wove false deny;
our greatest error, guilt. For what? We've arms and hearts and legs—
Aye, that we have! He cut me off, and breath with which to sigh.
To begin my life with the beginning of my life, I record that I . . .

And thence he shared his frightful tale of youth in Cornish mines,
of poverty and beatings, truths hard-earned, he had no prettiness,
not then or now, yet held himself broad open to the skies and to
the one across from him. I felt complete and beauteous and knew
that if he took me in his arms, the tight and cobbled patterns of
our world would ease—we'd fashion new mythologies, this day
of sweet desire I'd mark as testament, the sextant never erring in
my heart. We laughed the night to golden dawn upon the beach
he turned to me: But what of you, your life? My happiness, I'll say,
was born (as I have been informed and believe) on a Friday.

Quatrain Contributors

Half the fun of writing and editing glosas is getting to know the poets, prose writers, and philosophers who "loan" their quatrains or four lines for the opening stanza. As a short story writer and would-be novelist, I prided myself for years on poetic illiteracy, which isn't all bad because to discover poetry in early mid-life is like discovering chocolate or sex or snowboarding for the first time. Life suddenly blazes into whole new levels of unpredictability.

What follows are thumbnail sketches of the quatrain contributors in the order of their appearance in *Dead to Rights*. They're designed less to educate than to whet your appetite for more, or to remind you of those you loved to read and had forgotten. I encourage you to seek out their work on-line, in your local bookstore or library. I will bet you, dollars to donuts, that you will find that you already carry more poetry and more wisdom in your heart from these great minds than you thought you did. We quite literally would not be who we are, had they not been.

John Keats (1795-1821) is often known, as he was to me and other non-poetic types, as the middle syllable of "Shelley, Keats, and Byron." An English Romantic poet, his work was scarcely noticed during his lifetime, though he eventually became one of the world's most beloved and influential poets, analyzed in schools around the world. Jorge Luis Borges, the great Argentine poet and short story writer, described his initial encounter with Keats as the most significant literary experience of his life. John Keats, who'd suffered from ill health all his life, died of TB at age 25 in Rome.

William Blake (1757-1827), an English poet, painter, and printmaker, was considered a madman and a heretic in his day. His own illustrations of heaven and hell, dragons, demons and angels accompanied his bold poetic landscapes, both of which reached a new 20th century audience through Thomas Harris's Hannibal Lecter books and films. Blake was a visionary whose out-of-body experiences fueled his imagination. In fact, he viewed Imagination as both the Body of God and Human existence itself. "Tyger, tyger, burning bright" is only one tiny spark of the great luminary soul whose flame touches us all.

Rainer Maria Rilke (1875-1926) was a Bohemian-Austrian poet who wrote in German and French. His haunting portrayals of anxiety, depression and solitude distinguished him from the overwrought sentimentality of his peers; he is often considered the father of modernist poetry. Rilke suffered from severe depression for twelve years, unable to write a word, before bursting into poetic flow with the dazzling *Duino Elegies*. His most famous prose work, *Letters to a Young Poet*, offers an excellent introduction to Rilke if, like myself, you find the dive straight into his achingly beautiful poems too daunting.

Edgar Allan Poe (1809-1849) was an American author best known for his tales of mystery and the macabre, though he's perhaps best known for the poem that gained him instant literary fame, "The Raven". Poe is considered the father of modern detective fiction and by virtue of a little-known 40,000 word prose poem, "Eureka", a contributor to the emerging science fiction genre. He struggled with alcohol addiction and depression, brought on partly by the stresses of attempting to support himself full-time by writing. On the topic of crafting suspenseful page turners, this master still has much to teach us.

Friedrich Nietzsche (1844-1900) was a German philosopher and perhaps one of the most misunderstood thinkers of our time. The author of *Thus Spake Zarathustra*, his concepts include the death of God, Übermensch (Super or Overman), eternal recurrence and the will to power. He devoted his life to understanding what he believed was humanity's journey toward the state of Overman. Nietzsche encouraged us to challenge all doctrines that drain life's naturally expansive energies, so that we might generate our own will to power the life of our deepest choosing. In 1889, he suffered a complete mental collapse and spent his last eleven years being cared for by his sister.

Alfred, Lord Tennyson (1809-1892) As Poet Laureate of the United Kingdom during much of Queen Victoria's reign, Tennyson is perhaps best known for his exploration of mythological themes in works such as *Ulysses* and *Idylls of the King*. "Nature, red in tooth and claw", "'Tis better to have loved and lost/Than never to have loved at all," are a few of many phrases that have flowed from him into our collective consciousness. The unusual ordering of his name—I always feel obliged to pause at the comma—derives from his embarrassment over Queen Victoria granting him peerage. He wanted his beloved readers to know that he was still, underneath the baronial fluff and bother, their Alfred Tennyson.

Gavriel Navarro is the sole living contributor of a quatrain to *Dead to Rights.* The Spanish-born poet, musician and artist grew up in Venezuela and England, then spent eleven years in the Amazon as a hunter, an eco-tourist guide and apprentice to Piaroa shamans. He has published two collections of poetry, *The Wind and the Sea: Poems & Reflections on a Journey of No Return,* and *Fire and Earth: Poems & Reflections on the Nature of Desire,* and kindly allows Elaine Stirling, my biographer, to include his spirit self in *Dead Edit Redo.* Nothing, Gavriel would say, is as it seems. www.gavrielnavarro.com

William Butler Yeats (1865-1939) Playwright and theatre director, poet, politician, student of the occult, perhaps no one is harder to classify than the Irish-born Yeats. He won the Nobel Prize in Literature in 1923, the first Irishman to do so, and wrote his best work after the glory. His lifelong obsession with heiress and muse, Maud Gonne; his love for Ireland; friendships with Ezra Pound and Indian author and mystic Rabindranath Tagore, all were grist for his startling poetic imagery. *Turning and turning in the widening* *gyre/The falcon cannot hear the falconer/Things fall apart; the centre cannot hold*, he writes in "The Second Coming". Indeed, it cannot.

John Milton (1608-1674) A civil servant in the employ of Oliver Cromwell during a time of great religious and political upheavals, John Milton is best known for his epic poem *Paradise Lost*. Viewed from a 21st century lens, what's amazing is that this polemicist and man of letters lived a natural life span, given that the protagonist and narrator of *Paradise Lost* is Lucifer. A vociferous opponent of censorship, Milton spent several years as a fugitive and saw his writings burnt before influential friends helped obtain a pardon. He survived the Great Plague of London, married three times, the last to a woman half his age, and spent his final years writing peacefully.

Epictetus (55-135 CE) was born to slavery in present-day Turkey and grew to become a Stoic philosopher. Lame since childhood, he worked for Nero's personal secretary until he somehow obtained his freedom and was banished from Rome. He spent the remainder of his life in Greece, developing his philosophy of calm, dispassionate acceptance. All suffering, he believed, stems from our attempts to control what is uncontrollable and in neglecting to do what lies within our power. His Handbook, a collection of maxims, was compiled by a disciple; his true name is not known to us. Epictetus means "acquired" or "owned" in Greek.

Rumi (1207-1273) is enjoying a huge surge in popularity on Facebook and other social media sites, perhaps because of his quotability. Jalāl ad-Dīn Muhammad Balkhī, Mevlānā in Turkish, was a Persian mystic and poet who lived in Konya, Anatolia. An Islamic teacher and jurist, his life was transformed when he met Shams e-Tabrizi, a dervish who'd been awaiting his disciple all his life. Known for spontaneous public outpourings of ghazals, Persian verse, Rumi spent twelve years street-rapping six volumes of his master work, the Masnavi: his major theme, union with the Beloved, from whom we have cut ourselves off and yearn to return. His shrine in Konya is one of Turkey's most popular pilgrimage and tourist sites.

Saggil-kīnam-ubbib was a temple incantation priest circa 1700 BCE at a time when Sumerian and Akkadian were the principal languages in Mesopotamia, the land between the Tigris and Euphrates Rivers. Little is known of the author except for his profession, which includes the addendum , "adorant of the god and king." Creator of the first known acrostic poem, his work has been translated by W. G. Lambert and appears in *Babylonian Wisdom Literature*, published by Oxford University Press, 1960.

Enheduanna (2285-2250 BCE), the first known female poet, was an Akkadian princess and high priestess of the Moon god Nanna in the Sumerian city-state of Ur. Aunt of the Akkadian king Narām-Sin, she composed 42 hymns for temples across Sumer and Akkad, known collectively as "The Sumerian Temple Hymns". These have been reconstructed from 37 tablets and include the inscription: "My king, something has been created that no one has created before."

Her prayers to Inanna, Queen of Heaven and Earth, stand today among the finest exaltations to the feminine and the voluptuous.

Miguel de Cervantes Saavedra (1547-1616) was a Spanish novelist, poet and playwright, best known for his magnum opus, *Don Quixote*. Little is known of his early years, although it's believed his father was a barber-surgeon from Galicia who moved his family often to avoid creditors. Cervantes became a soldier with the Spanish Navy Marines, renowned for bravery with sword and gun. Captured by Algerian corsairs, he was enslaved for five years and later, spent long stretches in prison for indebtedness and offending authority. It was during these times of confinement that he wrote what has come to be known as the first modern European novel. Satirical and complex, *Don Quixote* earned its author great acclaim, opprobrium, and the worthy sobriquet, *El Príncipe de los Ingenios*, "The Prince of Wits".

John Donne (1572-1631) was an English poet whose mastery of metaphor, eroticism, satire and imagery, led him to be known as "the metaphysical poet". Though he developed a strong religious tone later in life, Donne's early work lambasts the Elizabethan court for its pomposity and mediocre use of English. His complex, paradoxical logic became its own literary device, known as conceits. Sylvia Plath, on a BBC Radio interview in 1962, said, "I remember being appalled when someone criticised me for beginning just like John Donne but not quite managing to finish like John Donne, and I felt the weight of English literature on *me* at that point." Donne, I suspect, would have told her to chuck off the weight and keep writing.

Herman Melville (1819-1891) is an American novelist, essayist, short story writer and poet whose name is indelibly linked with his most famous work, *Moby Dick*, and yet it was his first two novels, *Typee* and *Omoo*, that were the runaway bestsellers. After their publication, thirteen years passed, during which time he married, raised a family, and farmed in Massachusetts because book royalties were never enough to live on. To our good fortune, Melville's neighbour happened to be Nathaniel Hawthorne, author of *The Scarlet Letter* and *House of the Seven Gables*, with whom he shared tales of his whaling days. Melville dedicated *Moby Dick* to Hawthorne. Although the book was published both in the UK and US, it failed to sell out its initial print run of 3000 during his lifetime. The author of what has been called the greatest novel ever written died in obscurity at his home in New York.

Giacomo Casanova (1725-1798) Aah, dear Casanova! To be labeled an adventurer by 19th century historians was a title reserved for very few. It was code, of course, for "slept around" and his adventures with women made his name synonymous with the deed. Labels, however, also have the unfortunate power to blinker our ability to see beyond them. The Venetian-born writer was indeed a socialite, spending his days with luminaries such as Voltaire, Goethe, Mozart, and Benjamin Franklin. But he was also a keen observer of the social and political intrigues of 18th century Europe. He spent much of his life on the lam, running from powerful people he'd managed to insult. During his final years, exiled and bored, Casanova wrote twelve volumes of memoirs in French. In 2010, the French government began the prodigious task of digitizing the work in its entirety.

Charles Dickens (1812-1870) What can one say about this beloved Victorian novelist and social critic whose characters walk among us still, more real, at times, than ourselves? Oliver Twist, David Copperfield, Uriah Heep, and, of course, Ebenezer Scrooge: in total, he wrote fifteen novels and hundreds of short stories while maintaining a frantic lecture schedule and siring ten children. Known as "a literary colossus", he was also the world's finest serialist. Dickens published his great novels in installments that were read as quick as he could pen them, honing his craft to an inconceivable razor's edge. To rise from poverty to international acclaim, to write with such fervour that social institutions crumble and rise at the touch of your pen: this is what it means to have written.

ACKNOWLEDGMENTS

My thanks to PK (Patricia) Page for introducing me to the glosa years before I showed the slightest inclination toward verse or anything remotely disciplined. I am grateful to Tim C. Taylor for believing in this project, to Gavriel Navarro for his generous comments and critiques, and to Elaine Stirling for embracing the work and concepts of Fernando Pessoa. Perhaps, one day we will find that we are all heteronyms, one to another.

About the Author

Photo credit: Kara Bobechko

Alain C. Dexter is a professor of poetry at Brougham College and best-selling author of the award-winning *Gizzard's Luck & Other Organic Festivities,* a collection of short stories; the poetry collection, *Poems from the Soles of his Feet,* and two other collections of verse.

He is also a heteronym of the writer, Elaine Stirling. A concept introduced by the Portuguese writer and poet, Fernando Pessoa (1888-1935), who collaborated with more than seventy during his lifetime, a heteronym differs from a pseudonym in that the personage enjoys his/her own identity, writing and life styles.

Dexter enjoys imported beer, hiking in the great Canadian north woods, and hobnobbing with the rich and famous. He appears as himself in Stirling's novella of horror and good medicine, *Dead Edit Redo,* and lives on the north shore of Lake Superior.

Dead Edit Redo

Professor and best-selling poet Alain C. Dexter leaps to his death at Valletta Falls, moments after posting his final Facebook update, in the shape of a woman's breasts. Thousands of fans click *Like* and move on; only one, in a small Icelandic town, sees through the morbid wit and takes measures to save him. Meanwhile, Constable Elsie Kalahash of the Ontario Provincial Police just wants to go on holidays. But when you're a Cree medicine woman trained in the Backward-Facing Path, there are no days off.

Discover the story behind the glosas you have just read in this novella of horror and good medicine by Elaine Stirling. Available now from Greyhart Press.

Dead Edit Redo

A Novella of Horror

and Good Medicine

Elaine Stirling